Fantastic Feet!

Written by
Cath Jones

Illustrated by
Bryony Clarkson

There was a new shop on the high street.
A sign in the window said, "Fantastic Feet."

"Fantastic Feet! What an odd name," thought Clive.

"Come on," Gran said. "You need new Wellington boots."

When they went in, there was a fanfare of loud trumpets!

"Goodness!" said Clive. "Trumpets!"

"Welcome to FANTASTIC FEET!" called out an odd little man.

He looked about a hundred years old. He had a black cloak draped around his shoulders.

"Clive needs Wellington boots for a school trip," said Gran.

"We have lots of boots," said the man. "I will fetch some for you."

Gran sat down on a sofa to wait.

Clive set off to look around the shop.
There were stacks of boots everywhere.

He saw some gleaming cowboy boots in a dark corner.

"Put me on," they said to Clive in a whisper.
"Put me on now."

Clive could not resist!

When he put them on …

WHOOSH!

The boots leapt into the air – and so did Clive!

Suddenly, Clive was in a field next to a large horse.

There was no sign of the shop or of Gran.

The horse gave Clive a little nudge with its nose.

"I wonder if I should climb on?" thought Clive.

It was not easy to climb up, as the horse was so high.

As soon as Clive was on top of the horse, it set off at a brisk trot!

"Slow down," called Clive.
He began to panic. What was happening?

Then the horse broke into a gallop!

KER-THUMP!

Clive fell off …

… and found himself back in the shop!

Gran was fast asleep on the sofa.

"Did you find something fantastic?" asked the odd little man.

He grinned, as if he knew that Clive had been on an adventure.

Before Clive could reply, Gran woke up.

"I have some black Wellington boots," said the man.

"Thank you," said Gran. "They look just right."

The man gave Clive a second box. It was huge, with an elegant pink ribbon.

"You get an extra pair free," the man said with a wink.

Gran went and paid for the boots.

As they left, she said, "What an odd little shop!"

Clive took the box with the pink ribbon home.

"I wonder what fantastic footwear will be inside this box," he thought.